ACCIDENTAL GRACE

The publication of this volume
is supported in part with
funds from the National
Endowment for the Arts.

ACCIDENTAL GRACE

by

LUKE

Volume Six
in the Callaloo Poetry Series
Published at the University of Kentucky
Lexington, 1986

Some of the poems in this volume were published in three anthologies,
The Missouri Poets (Eads River Press), *Soda* (Quarter Press), and
Quickly Aging Here (Doubleday/Anchor); and in the following
periodicals: *America Magazine, Callaloo, New Orleans Review,
Ritual & Dissent,* and *Yardbird Reader #4.*

Cover design and art by Richard J. Powell

First Edition, 1986

ISBN: 0–912759–08–9

CALLALOO POETRY SERIES
University of Kentucky
Lexington, Kentucky 40506–0027

Contents

Part One

Lord Knows

lord knows honey
she said folding her hands
into the flowers of her apron
you got to make your
own road
                    sometime

it was her wisdom
so i waited

coming and going
aint gonna do
when you get to be
old like me   just
going
            aint it like
some folks   to jump
on their own backs
stead of using the road
to get somewhere   fools
is fools   but you aint never been
one you hear
                        sure gonna be hard
on your mama though
but she'll do all right
                                now
before you go i wants to give you
a little something
                        to help out
and i still have it

and the dollar bill
she unfolded slowly and put
into my hand

About a Month Ago

    about a month ago
               this ugly old
dog took up with us sleeping on
the front porch and following us
around with the most mournful
look
    nobody paid him no mind or
fed him or petted him
               we just
walked around him and ignored
him like some old grease smell
that stays and stays in the
kitchen
    after awhile i started
feeling kind of sorry for him

too old to move much he just
laid there i dont know maybe
he was too old to feel sorry
for and just wanted some peace
                 we
found that dog dead in the street
yesterday
     and i started looking
around this place thinking about
why i stay
    lord knows it cant be
my pedigree

Some Few, Some Very Few

some few, some very few, possess death
when it comes and hold onto it —
a daguerreotype displayed
next to their bed it becomes
a conversation piece referred to
as calmly as an ivory cameo bought
somewhere in switzerland

                    this old woman —
the link for me to quantrill's raiders and
strawberries stolen the summer of 1889 and
hunger kept
on dusty shelves —

this old woman
took death into her body years ago
with quiet hospitality she understood
its need and could not refuse
though this new expense would
exhaust her small resources

she was once a large woman
a matriarch whose authority grew complete
as she buried two sisters four brothers
mother father six of her children

husband   turned to the business
of her own funeral she has made
one last count of her household goods:
examined the soul of each survivor:
inventoried her life's decisions:
now she waits

while sewing a dress
from the remnant memories
of ninety years she says death
is cold to her: she does not like it

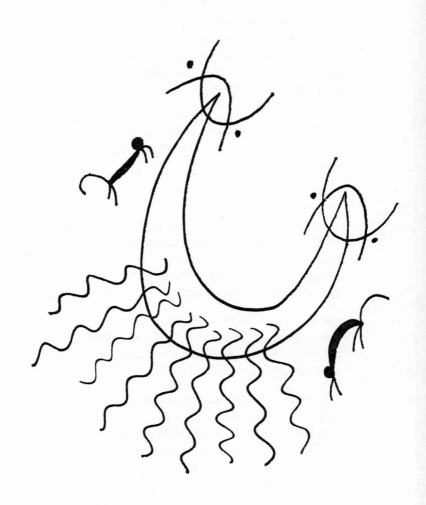

There Must Be a Source

there must be a source of music somewhere
that plays inside the heads of these young girls
who walk so
            softly   so softly
                        the long thin arms
moving easily with a slow swing brushing against
the also thin hard legs that partly pace
                        partly march
like cats brown black and soft young girls
with the firm look of untested flesh
                        that music
must be sad that they hear from somewhere
because they walk so softly and with a sureness
of time that no one ever learns but is with them
from somewhere
            and always
                        one of them plays
her woman game with a boy on the street and
there are no words just a moment made old
because her eyes tell him his body is good
and young and untested and he knows
                        and
she quietly easily softly slaps his face with
gentleness
            holding him to her for just a pulse
they are intimate and understanding here on
the corner and they both move to a music that
comes from inside
            a music that no one that young
could know
            which means that inside
they are old and it is another world that
has made them old
            and given them this music
which is soft   and it is sad

Into a Climb: For Pete

        when we arrived at the campsite
        a deep whisper came into our voices
        there at the west face of teewinot
        where the gros ventre had hunted
        eagles and starved themselves into
        warriors   you guided me   at last
        into your father's world
                            it was
        as if the shock of hard rock
        faces   and silences   and the final
        ascent became your father   while
        the mountains took his failings
        into their slides and decaying
        peaks
                into a climb you
        started at the age of five   past
        the treeline and glaciers   we look
        where the high country is flat
        yellow dust   where the country
        who is my father sits untended
        without words or whispers

At the Edge

my mother loses breath and nerve
as she watches my father resist all
aid and ease for death
                          his life is
devoured in larger doses daily with-
out the rescue
                    of imagination he is
letting go of sound and wit and
serenity
              believing it to be a game
of interference he will not narcotize
his pain and it spills
                          onto us all
restless angry impotent and vain to
dream what will never be   he pushes
us
      to dwell at the edge of a dwindling
fire a draining river and stare
her bewildered hands scream out and
grab her children
                        she would marry
him and bear his sons   she will
grieve when he is gone
                            but she cannot
rest hearing him now unable to replace
pain with peace
                      and she does not know
how to scold him to go to sleep for fear
that he would at last obey

Home Visit at Christmas

i wonder do you sit there for all
time   waiting to be seen in the light
we bring
            revealed in prophecy
uncovered by idle drunken sons
the shame of death   discovered
stranger   erasing your hardness
height and flesh
                        i look at your
hands
        hands that pulled us into
traffic   into crowds   curses
giants   monstrous shadows   all
too fierce and inarticulate
to withstand
                    except we were
pulled through them gently
roughly   with — at the last —
dispatch as each new son was
ready to be flung out into wind

the pattern stayed
the delicacy disappeared

your hands now tremble matches
drop bits and crumbs   ignore
the simplest string and button
lay soft and tired on your chair

if you would
motion to me now   this second
i would take your touch in gentle
gratitude
                but where could i take
you   what could i show you in this

world i still fear
                    and would you
come with me   if i asked
                        my nakedness
was your last great humor   yours has
become my penitence and drought

i am no guide for you
i cannot bear your gaze
your fading life brushes
across my heart and
drives
me into flight
                    you are mute
having packed your words away
and i am dumb   in need still
of my private roots
                    and
the children we hold between
us shake out our grasp so soon

Sentences of Christmas: A Novel

1. *(christopher :: william)*
christopher is my sister's child. christopher william.
and william is his great-grandfather. william christopher.
i knew him. he was born on christmas day

2. *(old)*
christopher william is new. in our family the youngest
in years is always new. to be grown by everyone.
to be told and shown in stories years that everyone
old saw and remembers. christopher remembers me.
i remember william. and so we are known.

3. *(but not for william)*
he sometimes runs to the door looking for me.
sometimes the door opens and i come through it.
sometimes he waits. waiting is new for christopher.
but not for william.

4. *(then she is new and she remembers)*
high born. born high. carried high by everyone so that
he could be shown what is known. and what is new.
laura is known as the wife of william   is old until
she sees christopher. then she is new and she
remembers. he has his eyes.

5. *(laura knows this)*
we are seldom known by what we see recognizing
is not knowing. laura knows this. she recognizes
death and christopher and she knows the difference.

6. *(this is what she remembers)*
christmas is the difference between every christmas and
william to be told and shown to christopher. when
he tells us and shows us that he knows it will be
new. this is what she remembers. she waits to tell william.

7. *(and he was carried high on christmas through a door)*
when christopher tells us that he knows we will remember
that it was new when william told us.   and he told us
all.   he had laura for the telling and he was carried
high on christmas through a door   a world of doors
every door that stood the telling.

8.   *(who was born on christmas)*
jesus comes into this now.   now everyone remembers.   who was
born on christmas.   everyone who remembers was born on
christmas.

9.   *(seldom known are the shadows until he can remember*
     the smell and sound and the grip of hands around
     his waist swinging him up with laughter)
of course the door we open for christopher is old.
seldom known are the shadows until he can remember
the smell and sound and the grip of hands around his
waist swinging him up with laughter.

10.   *(did the hills laugh)*
did the hills laugh.   laughter is as old as the hills.

11.   *(presents always bring laughter and scrambled heaps of paper)*
over this is the memory.   and each wrapped present.   christopher
brings william and laura a present.   he has their eyes and
their laugh.   presents always bring laughter and scrambled
heaps of paper.
                    he was always there.
                                        sometimes behind the door
sometimes opening it for us.   if you cannot remember that what
is the use of knowing and telling it again and telling it
again will you know it and remember it is remembering christmas
remember that brought us to this door where christopher
stands waiting for me and william and a world that is as yet

for him as new as laughter and told again when she recognizes
his eyes and the surprise of a life before him.

12.   *(that a child knows)*
and as he steps through the door she hands him
a life kept freshly wrapped in her mind seeing
in his young eyes the memory that a child knows.

13.   *(william and christopher)*
a child (william) (christopher) knows that again
christopher is william and each of us tells him
that we remember now we remember and we knowing
know that
        the one who is to come is here.

14. *(with jesus.   laughter)*
it has something to do with jesus it has some thing
to do with laughter.   some thing and everything to
do with jesus.   any child can see.   who knows.   and so
it is known

Part Two

an experience in which a personage, thing, or event appears
vividly or credibly to the mind, although not actually
present, under the influence of a divine or other agency:
a vision. does it always start with a vision? how long
must you wait before you can call it a vision? and what did
you see?

i saw myself sitting on the top of a high mountain,
with my back leaning against a brilliant moonwhite cross.
from the base of the mountain all the way up to the crest
line were thousands of people who were stretching towards
me. and i, sitting there spent, reached out my arms — as
a shadow of the cross — towards them.

and during the space
of one year, i saw this four times. and now when i think
of it, i see just as clearly as the first time it came to
me. was this the look of the still voice that socrates
heard? was this the chalice of jesus in gethsemane? was
it even a vision? how do you test it out? i have told
three experts about "my dream" and none of them ever gave
me more than a funny look and a long silence.

and we have
been trained to sort out even the silences in our lives.
so, if you please, distinguish. it was real. right. it
fits. it works. eight years of waiting has sifted the
hard, clean grains of my life. they exist. but are they
named? can they be named? of course they can be
named managed understood tamed. if we do it just do it
doing it always tames the unknown give god a name his future
is ours and we are his people. the words. magic is in
the words. always for me in the words. and the silence.
the long silence. to be broken. the silence? no. me.
i am to be broken. wasnt that an obvious clue to it all.
be broken. the hard grains of your life are sifted through
the silence. and you must be pieced out to be spilled.
and they will come and feed upon you. if your strength is

hard and clean and full of blood, the hungry will smell it
and come to eat. be the lamb of god. roasted. at least
properly dressed and quartered.

                            to perform the sacred rites
especially the sacrificial offerings. walk down the street
in north st. louis and that will be enough. call yourself
priest over cocktails and see. hunger and desperation.
the offering of sacrifice. even if you are imagining it,
when you say this is my body and this is my blood, the
identification stays. and stays and after all they were
your words that everybody heard. roasted lamb. of god
and of the people. god is everywhere. and so is hunger.
you saying so simplifies matters.
my talent is to die. but not cheaply. to die for the best
possible price. on a mountain for a crowd. lift up the
sins of the world. i have lifted them up. lift up your
heart. i have lifted it up on a spit. a tree branch forked
and spearsharp. lifted up. in silence. at last i can
name it. sursum corda. the witness of dying. the show
the ritual the teaching of the people to lift up their
hearts in hunger. at last i face the question which for
years has had no word to bring it flesh. what is my priest-
hood. to live the vision and be lifted up. by god. for
the people. my gift and my service is not to perform works.
no i was sitting beneath the cross. it is not to speak.
the poetry of this world is silence and the asceticism of
option that we cannot exercise. i can speak
therefore i will not. i can give life therefore i will
not. i can rule therefore i will not. i can construct an
answer that will satisfy therefore i will not.

                                  the gift of
knowledge that i have shared has been time. the only gift
an artist has is time and the magic of controlling time.
if you know me you cannot escape the twisted heart that is
broken by wine and heroin and loneliness. and the breaking

will point where it will where it must. the endurance of
never leaving the edge of the knife. choose life therefore
choose the vision. i offer in my hands the body of jesus
broken by chaos and fear devoured by hunger and lonely
nights. it is the gift that god placed before me and i have
taken it up and said this is my body and my blood. if
you will not touch it can you turn away. if you avoid the
gift will you live your vision. the poverty of this world
denies any choice in the matter. what the lord gives you
receive. change your diet or starve to death. evolve
and grow. choose life and be new. wine. hearts of flesh.
men. a man called and chosen from among men to offer
sacrifice. to offer men as sacrifice. to lift up what we
have been gifted.

what will i do. nothing. you need me
for nothing except priest. the priest for the sacrifice.
you are the sacrifice and someone must prepare you. and
you know it. the vision is yours. the people are all of
us. all of our building and striving will fail to satisfy
because we are not asked to build or construct. we are
asked to sacrifice and witness to lift ourselves up as
offering for the people. and how are we to do this. find
your heart and break it like bread and let them feed upon
it. for they are hungry. and will you survive. if you
remember who you are and why you were chosen. to be reminded
to accept time and cast off fear. the strength of our life
must be a vision. and do you have a vision. you have me
and all i have is the sense of a vision. so now we know.
now we have a word for it now we have the magic. begin.
please begin. we are masters of the ritual and we must
begin or no one will know.

Part Three

When the Eagle Flies: St. Louis

the only right time for jesus to walk
in this city would be on friday night
because that's when the people are so
sad and loud and running around
and jumping and dancing and scared
like hell that somebody will see that
they're scared and wipe them off the earth
with understanding   that jesus could
do some good
                    but he wont be walking
the streets in this town because from
what i hear it's not safe and there
are too many loudtalking niggers and
soursouled white folks for jesus to
get to and comfort even if he had
all the time in heaven which
is what this place needs and aint
and everybody   even jesus   knows it

Good Friday in Omaha: Night

flat white pills given out at the county
clinic will short circuit the pain
                                    from
the plate in the thigh to the busted knee-
cap down to the shattered ankle
                                    the flat-
iron hotel will for five dollars plus tax
let you sleep in a plain room for one night
not let you bathe
                        not give you clothes that
need no pins to be kept decent
                                    the happy cab
company will send a young black driver to pick
you up
            and relieve the need to slide back
down the hill   your arms too weak to push
and steady the castaway crutches from st.
vincent de paul
                        and i will turn off my tape
recorder's hurting sound   silence bessie
smith's lesson for tonight and listen to
you
        that much can be done   and with such
dispatch that it seems a shame no one
knows how to get you back to scottsbluff
no one knows how to speed your pension
papers up
                no one knows   except maybe for
bessie how to answer your last slurred
question
                what do you do in the meantime
what do you do in the mean time
                                    i don't
know how to sing you a blues   it was just
my night to be on duty

Photographs: Atlanta, 1980–1981

1.

in some parts of the city even the dirt
is tired
        shuffled over   stomped on
swept flat   hard as a gravestone
it does not give to the step
                  so
men grow tired from walking on it

their aching legs get heavy as the sun
lowers its own hot weight to their shoulders
bearing down
               bearing down   and the dirt
resists   throwing back the shadows it
drains of moisture and tint
                   remaining still
dry
    still hard
          and dry
              and implacable

2.

what trees there are   stretched thin
with hate   ignore each other
              distantly
offering the weakest of branch   the slightest
of shade   pitiless to childish claims
of flickering peace   refuge   and cover

no old men lean under them
to recollect their purpose and their breath
no old women strip the leaves and the bark
for medicine
          the trees disdain to line
the land   the fields   or the foothills of

the northern range
                like the sparse jagged
teeth of some mythic prowling jackal
                     the trees
make wide and slashing wounds wherever they rip
into the middle sky

3.
down there   beyond the fence was a creek
once
        where the thicker brush and the high
weeds seem close
                their closeness is the only
sign
the rain might stay for two or three days
just enough to glut their roots and give
a beggar's sustenance

the children will slip off there now and
again and come back scratched and scared

they have to learn themselves that lesson
since no yelling ever gets through

4.
nobody knows how old she really is

if there was a shade tree she wouldn't care
for it
        has to be moved into the sun so that
she can feel it on her eyes
                (they got cloudy
years ago)
        when you get near you can smell
the cinnamon and smoke and lye that mingles

in her sweat
                she sits there hours every day
fingering that rag until holes are worn into it
calls herself looking out for the children
                                        but
they slip away
                they slip away
                                leave here for
good

brought one boy back last month looking
like life had squeezed him hungry

she reached out and stroked his face
                                and smiled
a little
                it was about all the sign you could
expect

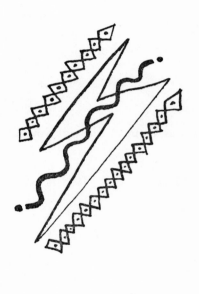

Stories About Chrone

i.

looks like chrone the care-
taker got careless
              again
when the lights went out last night
seems like he was rooting around
his junkroom and put in the wrong
size bulbs
           folks say chrone
ain't had his mind on duty since
his boy ran away and got killed
overseas (or down south
                 folks
ain't sure which as if it mattered
anymore)
           when you been here
awhile you learn to overlook his
crazy ways since they never hurt
nothing no way
              this time is rich
them lights make the whole neighbor-
hood look cleaner like they burn
some of the dirt away
             and the trees
look painted almost and the glare
is making the snow melt weeks
sooner than it ought to
             chrone
got the knack of messing in the
good with the crazy sure enough

ii.

ain't nobody never called him
nothing but chrone
           once my daddy

STORIES ABOUT CHRONE

said he found a letter dropped
by the doorstoop sent to mister
chronostheos eupater
                        daddy says
anybody called   chrono-the-os
you-payter must have a black
mama and a jew daddy
                        who else
would think up a name like that

some of us was sitting on
the roof talking about chrone
i don't believe he is the janitor
he really owns the place
                        and just
pretends to be a forgetful old
wino   i bet he's got money and
stuff everywhere
                        rotting and
stinking because he can't re-
member where he hid it
                              probably
saving it for his son and won't
admit his boy's been dead for
years
            they told me i was just
dreaming
                  i'm going to look
for it someday   somebody ought
to get some use out of it
                              cause
when chrone dies the government
will take it all anyway

chronostheos eupater: "God of time, the Benevolent Father."

iii.

i wonder why he wears a
wool sweater even on a hot
day
     my grandma said it's
just that he's old   older
than abraham
          and daddy said
yeah and he taught the snake
how to
     crawl
        and been cold
ever since

iv.

sitting here on the steps one
night the air pulled back
            like
when at supper everybody gets real
quiet because daddy's in one of his
moods liable to slap you silly if you
ask for water too loud
         and i had this
deep feeling of wanting to run off
some place alone
        when grandma started
singing one of her church songs in
the bedroom shouting she could sing
because she's happy
        and the air stretched
out and i stopped needing to run

just then the basement door cracked
open
     chrone didn't come out or move

or nothing
                    and i couldn't see him
through the space   so i sat there
and let grandma sing on in my head
it kept the night breathable
                              maybe
chrone had the same idea

Christmas: St. Louis

before you get the house in order   the tree-
lights untangled   and all your packages wrapped
and labelled   i thought i should write and tell
you that jesus was already seen this year by
a friend in the middle of a crowd at a stop-
light downtown

                    he was in a greyhound bus headed
for chicago

              my friend waved but jesus did not
seem to notice him he was staring at the sky
and he looked very tired and sad   my friend
said   we should let everybody know before they
waste a lot of time shopping and cleaning and
getting ready that jesus has come and gone
to another city

The Tomb of Ignatius: Rome

1.

mark it out: six footsteps. just under
that. deep enough for a child
for a child to hide and if able to stretch
and turn over it would touch the walls.
no more room.
not even air would be comfortable beyond
these limits. and tightly sealed.

2.

see it: a boat
a covered gold boat shaped
to float lightly into the sea riding
high off to the edge of nowhere
if called. or sent.

3.

angels everywhere. pulling the eye
up and around. pointing into corners where
prayer evaporates and silence lingers.
behind marble clouds and silver folds
bronze curving in and out the breath
that comes from holy places everywhere
you look. can you see it.
now. mark it. out.

4.

when the bones have been cleaned they must be
boiled until the last scraps of meat and muscle
collect on top. boil them in lye for the
best results

5.

results are seldom expected. even though
you know that plants need water

and rich dirt for successful growth   once
in awhile   a seed has been found
to take root in dust   airless dust
dust that is sealed away from
light   from rain   from everything but
memory
        (and even some times in forgotten
dust)

6.
we were wrong distracted   fools
after gold to believe that visions
come in silence
            through a busload of belgian
tourists buying postcards   avés riding
in a wave of mumbled music   timed by
camera shutters and lights locked in
15 minute cycles
          the vision in that should
have been a clue

7.
that he would have accepted

everything at once
how clear he knew that
not even bernini himself could contain
an italian determined on devotion

8.
little child
ignatius
who could follow a lame man
who wept more and more as
time slipped him somewhere.

beyond the child.
and back again

9.
called. or sent.
the eye cannot be held to silver
lights the perfect draping on an
angels thigh
              it is drawn to wonder
if the dust
has any hidden

10.
sustenance

11.
it could
it could

12.
something brought us here

13.
mark it. nowhere. mark it out.
see. somewhere. see it. dust.
gold and bronze. tears. visions.
called it. out.
              sustenance.
sent. sent or called. called.
and sent. sent and called. here.
yes here. of course here. he
would know.
              he knew. a flame
is always certain.
                    especially

in darkness. in silence. here.
yes here.
                sustenance. in dust.
in tears. in tourists. lights.
and visions. yes. mark it.
everywhere.

Evening News: St. Louis

willard wirtz, secretary of labor,
supports humphrey the news says
over in central illinois
the big muddy was reported
to crest safely under flood level
because of recent heavy rains
snow flurries with slight precipitation
were predicted for st. louis
johnson received an ovation
in st. patrick's cathedral
a late bulletin announced
that martin l. king was shot
to death tonight on a balcony
in memphis
there were 3,238 vietcong
killed last month by allied forces
mrs. mabel burnham won $630
in the kxok easter egg contest
the pope still declines to make a statement
on birth control

4 april 1968

Part Four

Upon Which to Rejoice

A slight stirring darkness
ordered us to hesitate.
Somehow we had found it.
The hard earth was matted with brittle hay;
the soaked-in acid smell of animals
stifled us in the first instants;
rough branches of juniper
scratched against the mud walls.
The night was cadenced
with the warm, heavy breathing
of a woman who has borne a son
and, resting from her labor,
looks upon her child.

We had not surprised them
or disturbed their night.
Unmistakably
they had expected us and we,
in turn, had sensed they would be there.

No one spoke,
which made the stillness reverence;
while provision for her comfort
became our awkward male concern:
adding to the fire, another cloak,
tethering animals. He took
our embarrassment with gentle
eyes and helped us do again
what he had done before we came.

But we had nothing else to give
and our silence was inadequate,
though none of us knew why.

A Legend of Caravans

as if the human mind could not hold
the shock of wise men worshipping
the irony was molded into a legend
of caravans led by kings
                              and we
could be content with gold
and the smoke of rich spices except
the equal play of chance in myth
gave to one   the blackness of night
to wear as he knelt before a cave
offering a judgment
                              (for one who would be
king who would be wise   who must be
god and man to hold the heavy
weight of gold   to savor adoration)
knowing his was the last
the bitterness gift   of sorrow

Deliver Into Us

St. Louis, 1971. The Search for Charles Hale

first in rain   then snow   through the fire-
chewed ruins of the northside deserted by
everything but cold rotting air
                         police and
city volunteers hunt for a missing child
                             keeping
us informed   to nothing definite   the news reports
feed our strained hope with some slight signs
each day
             and each night   the ageless silence
that is always with us   scratches our minds
like a desert wind   and we   like forgotten
nomads scattered in some dark countryside crawl
close and cling to whatever light we have
                             visited
with this   the listening city stirs before it
sleeps   waiting restless   without peace
distracted   and caught in time
                        until this child
is found   declared seen   or delivered into us

Saul's Daughter

"Michal the daughter of Saul . . . saw King David leaping and dancing before Yahweh and she despised him in her heart . . . ."

The scribbling dogs pretended a chronicle
of your deeds wherein I live a bitter woman
who laughed deriding your foolish ways

had I been given a spear   sweatsoaked naked
wonder
        it would have found what Saul my father
sought
       your heart

           nor was he mad with prophecy
as they describe it   the howling came like acid
he drank each time you curved your spine
into the music
        holding that ungainly harp like
the breath of god
        but you were ever negligent
of the eyes which were your true anointing
the old fool Samuel pushed you into sunlight
when   seeing   the sweat and oil of sheep
he stumbled to touch you   mumbling   fate

every stone in your sling since then has killed
me

your curse came not because of my laughter
radiance of Israel   promise of the people
a sun unto yourself   leaping   thrusting
into the air of God   glistening with frenzy
you have found the safest lover of your life

what denial could not do I cannot care

46

Saul went mad when Jonathan became your harp
played and feathered by your breath
Saul went mad with hope
                      thinking I would be
the vessel of your pride

let Michal be one night of Jonathan and I am
satisfied
           and I was
                    that one night of Saul's
pretending peace

again he hurled a spear wanting yours
to cut him clean and aching

the women and the boys say you ravaged the sky
in weeping Jonathan's farewell
                      no one spoke
of joy   locked inside the hungry daughter
of mad Saul the prophet   king   late of Israel

I had seen your cursing eyes enough by then
to know I lived secure
                  the princess   queen
of Israel will not weep because of dust
flung into her face
                  by your hot and stinking
dance
        Michal will be remembered
                      it was I
who turned your song to the sword my hands
would pull

your God who needs the souvenirs of men
to feed his vengeance
                has all of you now

stand there trembling   David of the harp
the music of your heart is his   your blood
his
        the milk of your hot beauty
                                no one need
love you more

and the blood and flesh of Jonathan and Saul
are mine
            beyond you by your truth
                                I despise
myself no more

Part Five

Part Five

The Arch: St. Louis

1.

we are coming back to it
the taste of cold air edged like
a blade, bitterness slicing
our throats   lancing our eyes
of salt
        drawing off the heart
the last film of hope we suffered
under
       the death of men
the rooting of despair in the few
(even the world is few when one
man you have known lifts his head
finally away from you
             and is silent
forever)
       survivors locked in trying
to understand

2.

the crying is heard whenever a shadow
resists the need for sun
the crying is felt in the muscles along
the back, the neck, the arms held ready
to lift, to hold, to take away
             (even
the world, if known, is lifted when one
man is carried into the earth)
             our last
link   desperately clung to for difference

3.

and yet
our hearts continue beating
the icy breath gulped in anguish
feeds the blood

and allows us the strength to stumble
until we are able
to walk

4.
we are coming back to it
we are coming back to it
we are coming back

5.
the sleeping spirit surges
up like oil

6.
we are all coming
back to it
it is all coming back

7.
those who possess the city sought
to claim their right forever
                    and
pulled out of the earth out of
the flat land/breasted river
                        the
silver ribbon
            to tremble in
the reflected moonlight and muddy
brown water

8.
no flags are left
from the north the river brings whispers
it is the whisper of the return
it is the shaking loose of dirt by skeletons
of the hunt

9.
for the voice of the spirit

Silas Blue Eagle of Rosebud

He is chief
             only in the summer
     when tourists
               come to strip his headdress
        and dangle the feathers
             from their rear-view mirrors

     The chamber of commerce
                  can verify
    his lineage
        (and do so
      on the back of a postcard)

The blood of Sitting Bull and Red Cloud
    has been tamed
            they say
    and the chief
      will pose for pictures
              every morning
for a very slight fee

For a Friend Returning to Rosebud Reservation

if you cannot explain your return
they will not teach you   it is not
their way
                    they will invite you   and
sit with you   walking in the fields
at sunset they will notice you
stumble hungrily in the canyons
they will move aside
                              parting like
wind in the pine clusters they will
touch you
                    yes that is their way
touching
                    did you think that you
took nothing away when you left
before   did you remember the
whistling in the darkness   the
water rustling in the lake
                                        did
you find the thin purple and the
grey mist and the sand brown light
driving on any highway into the
west or south
                         the sand scratched
at your skin   the air stuck to you
and the empty sky cleared your
vision
                    they will not teach you
they will wait for you staring and
smiling   singing the wordless songs
offering you space
                              they will wait
for you to be chilled inside your
lungs and ask for a place near

the burning fire
                    they will not
teach you   but they will give you
time enough to learn how
                              the hills
slide into the river without fear

The Priests of Rosebud

have an accidental grace to no
longer fear the circle of their
beginning
to know the people of these plains
in courtesy   not wrath

but there is a curse with power in
the wind and rain and thunder

to die for what they believe
would be a blessing
to beg browbeat or threaten god
for signs and wonders   would make
them heirs of the golden-colored
saints that hang upon their walls

but the connection has died within
them
        these priests are orphans
of their history
                the people will
not kill them   the people look
away to salvage their pride

the people give them gifts
of crowd and circumstance

this new martyrdom is the losing
of the center   the absence of an
end to doubt   the daily taste
of smallness
                the people stay fixed
and the priests of rosebud move from
place to place praying for deliverance

The Burial of Pearl Walking Eagle at Rosebud

wide standing clouds held still
by the dakota sun offer me no shade
strings of heat web   weave and hook
a net that catches us struggling
like fish pulled   gasping for air
from the sea
                        and so we do not move
arranged as lodge poles around
the gravesite   we are attentive
in our steaming silence
                                    the wind
is soft and warming   the ground
is hot   the grass where it grows
among the gravel and the sand
defies the dryness

the walking eagle woman
                                    is free
of us   and is burdened now by
only the mound of earth and
plastic flowers
                        for nothing
flourishes here but resignation

wild heaped and brittle splotches
the flowers will not die
they will not fall   (the air is
much too gentle)
                        i learn that
reverence stands still
                                    and the
sharp keening of her daughter is
the only prayer with the power
to cut through us all and beyond
the vast prairie to breaks
without an echo

ABOUT THE AUTHOR

JOSEPH A. BROWN, SJ, was born in East St. Louis, Illinois, in 1944. After graduating from high school, he entered the Society of Jesus (the "Jesuits"), a Roman Catholic religious order. Brown attended Marquette University, St. Louis University, Johns Hopkins (The Writing Seminars), and Yale University, where he received the Master's degree in Afro-American Studies and the Ph. D. in American Studies. Brown taught drama and poetry at Creighton University in Omaha, Nebraska, for several years after his ordination to the Roman Catholic priesthood in 1972. He is presently an Assistant Professor in English and Religious Studies at the University of Virginia.

ARTIST AND COVER DESIGNER

Richard J. Powell, artist and critic, studied at Morehouse College and Howard University. He taught art courses at Norfolk State before beginning his doctoral studies at Yale University, where he has specialized on the life and work of the Afro-American painter, William H. Johnson.